PHARAOHS
& MUMMIES

ANITA GANERI

Consulting Editor
Peter Clayton

PRESENTATION 1996 BY LADYBIRD BOOKS, NEW YORK

A QUARTO CHILDREN'S BOOK

Copyright © 1996 Quarto Children's Books Ltd,
The Fitzpatrick Building,
188–194 York Way,
London N7 9QP

First published in the United States 1996 by Ladybird Books,
a division of Penguin Books USA Inc.,
375 Hudson Street, New York, NY 10014

ISBN 0-7214-5628-6

Creative Director Louise Jervis
Senior Art Editor Nigel Bradley
Editor Simon Beecroft
Paper Engineer Geoff Rayner
Picture Manager Vicky King

U.S. Editorial
Consulting Editor Dr. James Romano, Department of Egyptian Art,
Brooklyn Museum, Brooklyn, New York

Illustrators
Julian Baker, Madeline David, Kevin Jones Associates, Roger Stewart

Picture Credits
a = above, *b* = below, *c* = center, *r* = right, *l* = left, *of* = outside flap, *uf* = under flap
Ace Photo Agency: *Mike Tate* 2 / *Roger Howard* 19*of*; British Museum: 4*bl*, 5*al*, 5*bl*, 6*ar*, 7*bl*, 11*uf*, 14*ar*, 14*bl*, 15*ar*, 16*br*, 17*ca*; Peter Clayton: 8*cl*, 10*cl*, 11*bl*, 12*b*, 13*al*, 13*ar*, 13*cl*, 15*al*, 15*cl*, 16*ar*, 16*cr*, 16*bl*, 19*al*, 19*uf*, 20*cr*, 20*bl*, 22*al*, 23*al*; The Griffith Institute, Ashmolean Museum: 20*ar*, 20*cl*, 20*uf*, 20*of*; The Mansell Collection: 11*of*; James Putnam: 17*ar*

Manufactured by Bright Arts Pte. Singapore
Printed by New Island Printing Co Ltd, Hong Kong

Words that appear in **bold** are explained in the glossary on page 24.

CONTENTS

THE GIFT OF THE NILE

More than 5,000 years ago, a spectacular civilization flourished in Egypt. Most of the country was – and is – desert, too dry and dusty to farm or live in. But along the banks of the Nile River, the people found a precious resource that sustained them. Each year, the Nile flooded its banks, leaving behind rich deposits of silty, black soil.

From this fertile soil, farmers grew bountiful crops of wheat, barley, vegetables, and fruits such as grapes and pomegranates. They also raised cattle, sheep, and goats. A visiting Greek, named Herodotus, described Egypt as the "gift of the Nile."

Below *Wealthy Egyptians enjoyed hunting waterfowl, such as geese and ducks, and other river animals in the marshes along the Nile River.*

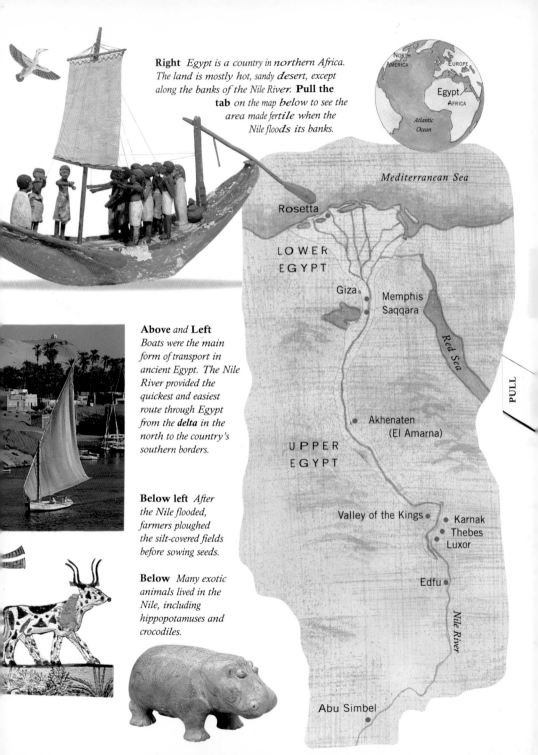

Right *Egypt is a country in **northern** Africa. The land is mostly hot, sandy **desert**, except along the banks of the Nile River.* **Pull the tab** *on the map **below** to see the area made fer**tile** when the Nile floo**ds** its banks.*

NORTH AMERICA

EUROPE

Egypt

AFRICA

Atlantic Ocean

Mediterranean Sea

Rosetta

LOWER EGYPT

Giza

Memphis
Saqqara

Red Sea

PULL

Above *and* **Left** *Boats were the main form of transport in ancient Egypt. The Nile River provided the quickest and easiest route through Egypt from the **delta** in the north to the country's southern borders.*

Akhenaten (El Amarna)

UPPER EGYPT

Below left *After the Nile flooded, farmers ploughed the silt-covered fields before sowing seeds.*

Valley of the Kings

Karnak
Thebes
Luxor

Below *Many exotic animals lived in the Nile, including hippopotamuses and crocodiles.*

Edfu

Nile River

Abu Simbel

PHARAOHS AND PEOPLE

T he Egyptian king was thought to be a god in human form, and his title, **pharaoh**, meant "Great House," or palace. He was the most important and powerful man in the kingdom. To keep the royal blood pure, the pharaoh often married a close female relation, such as his sister or half-sister.

Above *Ramesses II, shown in this statue, ruled Egypt from 1279 to 1212 B.C. He was a brave warrior and a great builder of temples and monuments.*

Social Pyramid

Egyptian society was arranged like a pyramid. The pharaoh was at the top. Then came the upper classes of high priests and nobles, followed by priests, government officials, and army generals. The next layer was larger and included merchants, craftsmen, and soldiers. At the bottom were the largest group, the laborers and peasants.

Left *The pharaoh wore a Blue War Crown in battle.*

CROWNING GLORY

Left *On ceremonial occasions, pharaohs often wore false beards.*

Pull the tab to see how the White Crown of **Upper Egypt (above)** was combined with the Red Crown of **Lower Egypt** to form a single crown after King Menes joined the two lands in about 3100 B.C.

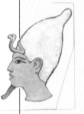

PULL

6

Above *After a sumptuous feast, wealthy Egyptians were entertained by musicians, as well as dancers and storytellers.*

Pharaohs' Duties

As well as having religious duties, pharaohs had to maintain law and order, protect the temples, and lead the Egyptian army. They also made peace treaties and alliances with other lands. Pharaohs often married foreign princesses to strengthen alliances – as a result some pharaohs had a great many "official" wives!

Above *Vases like this were used to hold perfume made from aromatic oils.*

Left *A wooden model of a servant girl carrying a tray of cakes. She is shown wearing black eyeliner, which was popular in Egypt. It was made of ground minerals, such as malachite (green) or galena (black), mixed with oil. Both men and women wore make-up, as well as jewelry.*

TEMPLE GLORIES

Egyptian **temples** were believed to be the earthly home of a particular god or goddess. Ordinary people were not allowed inside to worship. Only priests, priestesses, and the pharaoh himself were admitted.

Below *The Great Temple at Abu Simbel, built by Ramesses II, was carved out of a cliff facing the Nile. Four huge seated figures of the Pharaoh flank the entrance.*

Pleasing the Gods

The priests' main duty was to tend the statue of the god or goddess housed in the temple. They bathed and dressed it daily, and gave it food as if it were alive. They sang and prayed as they made their offerings. Then, when they departed, the priests swept the floor to hide any trace of their presence.

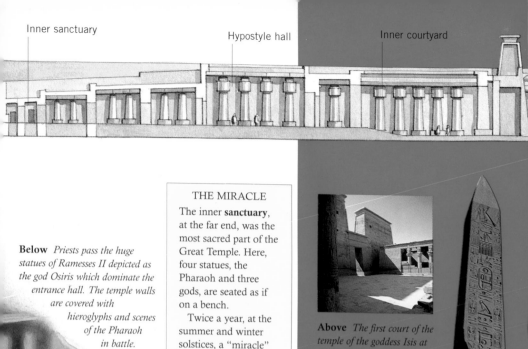

Inner sanctuary   Hypostyle hall   Inner courtyard

Below *Priests pass the huge statues of Ramesses II depicted as the god Osiris which dominate the entrance hall. The temple walls are covered with hieroglyphs and scenes of the Pharaoh in battle.*

THE MIRACLE

The inner **sanctuary**, at the far end, was the most sacred part of the Great Temple. Here, four statues, the Pharaoh and three gods, are seated as if on a bench.

Twice a year, at the summer and winter solstices, a "miracle" occurs. As the sun rises in the sky, sunlight shines across the temple floor and lights up the statues.

Above *The first court of the temple of the goddess Isis at Philae is found behind the massive entrance pylons. Isis represented the perfect mother.*

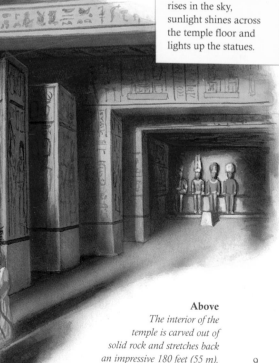

Above
The interior of the temple is carved out of solid rock and stretches back an impressive 180 feet (55 m).

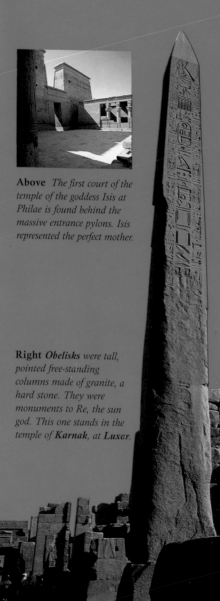

Right *Obelisks were tall, pointed free-standing columns made of granite, a hard stone. They were monuments to Re, the sun god. This one stands in the temple of **Karnak**, at **Luxor**.*

9

LANGUAGE AND LEARNING

T he ancient Egyptians were among the very first people to write things down. To do this, they invented a system of picture writing called **hieroglyphs.** Each hieroglyph, or picture, stood for a particular object or a sound.

Above *Ancient Egyptians wrote on paper made from papyrus reeds that grew along the Nile. Touch this piece of papyrus.*

School for Scribes

Hieroglyphs were complicated to use. **Scribes** spent years at special scribe schools learning how to read and write them.

Above *The hieroglyphs are still visible on the papyrus sheet held by this four-thousand-year old wooden scribe.*

Left *A typical scribe's writing box contained reed pens, ink blocks, and ink wells.*

Above *The hieroglyph for "writing" is a scribe's red and black ink wells, shoulder strap, water bottle, and pen case. Next to a hieroglyph of a person, this means "scribe."*

Hieroglyphs were not used for everyday matters, but for important inscriptions on tombs, temples, and for official documents. A simpler, shorthand style of writing called **hieratic** was used in daily life.

Above *Two scribes hard at work. Scribes held their hands above the surface of the papyrus to avoid smudges.*

Left *In this painted statue, a scribe sits in the traditional cross-legged position, with a papyrus scroll unfolded on his lap.*

A B C D E

H I J K L

O P Q R S

K(C) L I(E) O P A D(T

Cleopatra was Queen of Egypt from 51-her name in hieroglyphs. If you and yo the hieroglyphic alphabet, then you can messages to each other.

THE LANGUAGES OF THE ROSETTA STONE

HIEROGLYPHS

DEMOTIC

GREEK

WAGING WAR

T he pharaoh was not only the supreme ruler of Egypt, but also commander-in-chief of the Egyptian army. He often led battles himself.

Right *The handle of this dagger is topped with sparkling rock crystal.* **Lift the gold scabbard** *to see the iron blade. Iron was far rarer than gold in ancient Egypt. This is the only iron dagger to survive.*

Military Might

During the **Old Kingdom**, Egypt's small army was made up of foot soldiers armed with spears, bows and arrows, and shields. Untrained men were hired in an emergency.

Below *King Tutankhamun, standing in his war chariot, leads the Egyptians into battle against the Syrians, who lived in a land situated east of Egypt. The King wears the ceremonial war crown.*

In the **Middle Kingdom**, Egypt began conquering lands such as Nubia, which lay in the south.

Left *On this ivory seal, the Pharaoh Den (shown on the left) is about to strike an Asiatic soldier, from the deserts to the east.*

Right *These model soldiers carry spears and shields made of leather and wood. Wooden armies were placed in **tombs** to accompany the dead in the afterlife.*

Below *Egyptian soldiers (shown on the right) battle bearded Syrians, in this temple wall carving.*

Lift the flap *to see how this shield fitted onto a soldier's arm.*

During the **New Kingdom**, Egypt expanded northeast, conquering Syria and Palestine. With riches plundered from these lands, the army was reorganized and expanded. New weapons and body armor were introduced, and horse-drawn war chariots were used for the first time.

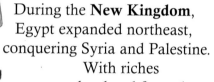

Right *Egyptian soldiers sometimes wore armor made of bands of tough leather. Weapons were made of bronze and wood.*

Far right *This bronze sword, with a deadly sickle-shaped blade, was discovered in the tomb of King Tutankhamun.*

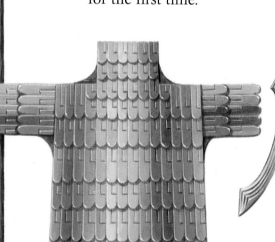

EVERLASTING LIFE

The ancient Egyptians believed in life after death. They thought that a dead person's soul traveled to an underworld, called ***Duat.*** There it underwent a series of trials and ordeals to reach the next world, called the Kingdom of the West.

Above *Amulets, such as this heart scarab, were placed between the bandages of a mummy for protection in the afterlife.*

Saving Souls

To insure that the soul enjoyed eternal life in the next world, the body of the dead person was preserved by a process called mummification. Many Egyptian **mummies** were so well preserved that they are still intact today.

MAKING A MUMMY

Lift the page to see how mummies were made. ❶ Internal organs were removed. ❷ The body was preserved with strong salt. ❸ Fragrant ointments were rubbed in. ❹ Finally, it was wrapped in bandages.

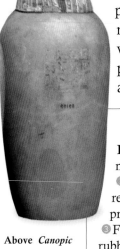

Above *Canopic jars held the internal organs of the dead.*

It is even possible to see what individual Egyptians looked like – or, rather, how they wished to be remembered for eternity.

Wealthy Egyptians were buried in ornamented coffins in decorated **tombs**. The mummies of poorer people were buried in simple holes in the hot desert sand.

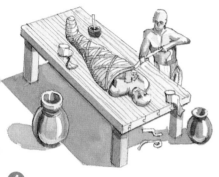

THE GODS OF ANCIENT EGYPT

T he ancient Egyptians worshiped hundreds of gods and goddesses who controlled all aspects of daily life and the forces of nature. Some were known throughout Egypt; others were sacred to certain towns. Some gods were worshiped over the centuries; others were replaced by new gods.

AKHENATEN

Akhenaten was the first king to worship just one god – the Aten, or sun god. He built a new city to honor his god. After the King died, people began to worship many gods again.

King of the Gods

The most important god during the Old and Middle Kingdoms was Re, the sun god. In the New Kingdom, he merged with Amun, the king of the gods, to become Amun-Re.

Left *The bull god, Apis.*

Left *Cats were sacred in ancient Egypt because they were associated with the cat goddess, Bast. The penalty for killing a cat was death. Dead cats were often mummified and buried in cemeteries.*

Right *The ibis bird was sacred to the scribe god, Thoth.*

16

EIGHT GODS AND GODDESSES

Turn the wheel to see eight of the most important gods in ancient Egypt.

The gods created the world, so the ancient Egyptians believed it was their duty to live according to the gods' will.

Turn the wheel to see eight of the most important gods in ancient Egypt.

Below *The falcon-headed sun god, Re, hands the ankh sign – the symbol of life – to Pharaoh Ramesses II.*

The Divine Image

Many gods and goddesses were depicted carrying objects that showed their sphere of influence: Thoth, the god of scribes, carried a reed pen. Others were shown with animal heads – for example, Anubis, the jackal-headed god of embalming. Animals associated with particular gods were often themselves considered divine.

Above
The eye of Horus was believed to be a lucky amulet with the power to protect everything behind it.

Left *Sekhmet, the goddess of war, is shown with the head of a lioness. She was the wife of the creator god, Ptah.*

Powers of the Gods

The gods created the world and governed everything in it. Egyptians had to follow their sense of *ma'at* (the ideal of truth and justice) by obeying laws and customs, working hard, and, for a King, ruling wisely.

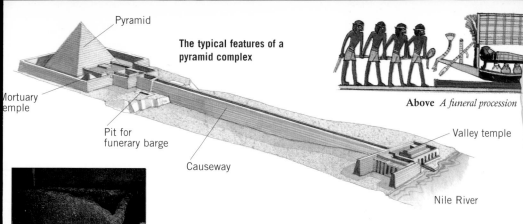

The typical features of a pyramid complex

Pyramid

Mortuary temple

Pit for funerary barge

Causeway

Valley temple

Nile River

Above *A funeral procession*

Above *King Khufu's stone coffin, or **sarcophagus**, stood in the King's Burial Chamber deep within the Great Pyramid.*

Below
No one knows for sure how the pyramids were built. Some experts think the stone blocks were dragged up a series of spiral ramps.

Back of acetate *The entrance of the Great Pyramid ➏ led to an unfinished chamber at the end of a descending corridor ➐. A second, ascending corridor ➎ leads through the Grand Gallery ➍ to the King's Chamber ➋. The so-called Queen's Chamber ➌ may originally have been intended for King Khufu. Ventilation shafts ➊ run from the chambers to the surface.*

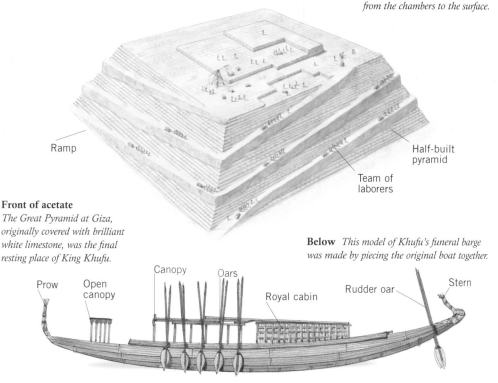

Ramp

Half-built pyramid

Team of laborers

Front of acetate
The Great Pyramid at Giza, originally covered with brilliant white limestone, was the final resting place of King Khufu.

Below *This model of Khufu's funeral barge was made by piecing the original boat together.*

Prow

Open canopy

Canopy

Oars

Royal cabin

Rudder oar

Stern

THE TOMB OF TUTANKHAMUN

The pyramids were easy targets for looters. Later pharaohs, therefore, were buried in underground tombs in the **"Valley of the Kings."** In 1922, British archaeologist Howard Carter found the superb tomb of Pharaoh Tutankhamun. Sealed for over 3,300 years, the first sight to greet the team was an anteroom filled with magnificent treasures.

Above *Howard Carter and his team open the* **shrine** *doors.*

Open the doors *(from the burial shrines) to see the array of treasures discovered by Howard Carter in the anteroom.*

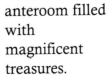

Above right *This pendant is made of gold and semi-precious stones.*

Left *Tutankhamun emerges from a lotus flower as a sun god, in this wooden sculpture.*

Right *Behind the sealed doorway of the anteroom lies the burial chamber containing the sarcophagus and mummy of Tutankhamun.* **Open these doors** *to see what lies behind.*

THE FACE OF THE KING

Far left *This statue of the goddess Isis is one of four that guarded the King's internal organs.*

Left *Isis spreads her winged arms on the inner side of the doors of this shrine.*

Above *A gold statuette of Tutankhamun*

Beyond the anteroom, in the Burial Chamber, lay the greatest discovery of all – the mummy of King Tutankhamun. It lay within a nest of three coffins, which were themselves protected by a stone sarcophagus and four gilt wood shrines. The pharaoh's face was also covered by an exquisite golden mask.

Right *One of Tutankhamun's thrones, made of ebony and inlaid with glass, ivory, and semi-precious stones*

Another small room led off from the burial chamber – the treasury. It housed the most valuable jewels and objects, including the King's throne.

Left *This collar is adorned with scarab beetles and cobras resting on the king's golden ship.*

Below *The three coffins ❶, ❷, and ❸ that contained Tutankhamun's mummy fitted inside each other like a Russian doll. The mummy itself wore a golden mask ❹. All three coffins rested within a huge sarcophagus made of a stone called quartzite.*

Below *This seal belonged to one of the officials who originally sealed the tomb over 3,300 years ago.*

Front and back of acetate *The first two coffins are made of gilt wood inlaid with glass and semi-precious stones.*
Left *The mask that covered the mummy's face is made of solid gold inlaid with semi-precious gems.*

4

GLOSSARY

Archaeologist Someone who studies the past by investigating surviving remains.

Book of the Dead A collection of prayers, spells, and information to help the dead in the afterlife.

Canopic jar A container that held the internal organs (stomach, liver, lungs, and intestines) removed from the body of the deceased.

Delta The marshy area in the north of Egypt where the Nile River flows into the Mediterranean Sea.
Duat The land of the dead, where souls were judged. If the dead person had led a good life, according to *ma'at*, they would travel to everlasting life in the "Kingdom of the West." Otherwise, the person's soul was eaten by a female monster called the "Eater of the Dead."

Hieratic The earliest shorthand form of hieroglyphs.

Hieroglyphs The Egyptian writing system that used images to convey both sound and meaning.
Hypostyle hall The large, many columned hall in most Egyptian temples.

Karnak The biggest and richest temple by the Nile, dedicated to the god, Amun-Re.

Lower Egypt The kingdom situated in the delta of Egypt.
Luxor Modern city on the east bank of the Nile. In ancient times, the city of Thebes stood here.

Ma'at The principle of truth and justice.
Middle kingdom (*c.* 2040 – 1750 B.C.) The second of three great periods of ancient Egyptian history, during which the temple of Karnak was begun and Egypt conquered the land of Nubia in the south.
Mummy The preserved body of a dead person or animal.

New Kingdom (*c.* 1550 – 1086 B.C.) Third great period of ancient Egyptian history. Pharaohs Akhenaten, Tutankhamun, and Ramesses II all reigned during this period.

Obelisk Tall, square-based stone needle put up at the front of temples.
Old Kingdom (*c.* 2613 – 2160 B.C.) First great period of ancient Egyptian history, during which the pyramids at Giza were built.

Pharaoh Egyptian word for king. It comes from the two words "per" (house) and "aa" (great).

Rosetta Stone A black basalt stone found in 1799 at Rosetta. Three identical texts appear on it – hieroglyphs, Demotic, and Greek.

Sanctuary The small inner room of a temple where the sacred statue of the god stood.

Sarcophagus Stone outer coffin that held a mummy inside decorated wooden coffins.
Scribe A highly trained person who could read and write hieroglyphs.
Sphinx The Great Sphinx at Giza is a huge statue of a lion with a human head that stands next to the pyramid of King Chephren.
Shrine The chamber containing a god's image, usually placed within the sanctuary.

Temple A place where gods are worshiped.
Tomb A place where dead bodies are buried.

Upper Egypt The southern part of Egypt. It took control of Lower Egypt. The two kingdoms merged to form one nation.

Valley of the Kings Hilly region situated on the west bank of the Nile at Luxor where New Kingdom Pharaohs were buried in tombs.